MAKING CANDLES

Written by Judy Ann Sadler

Illustrated by Tracy Walker

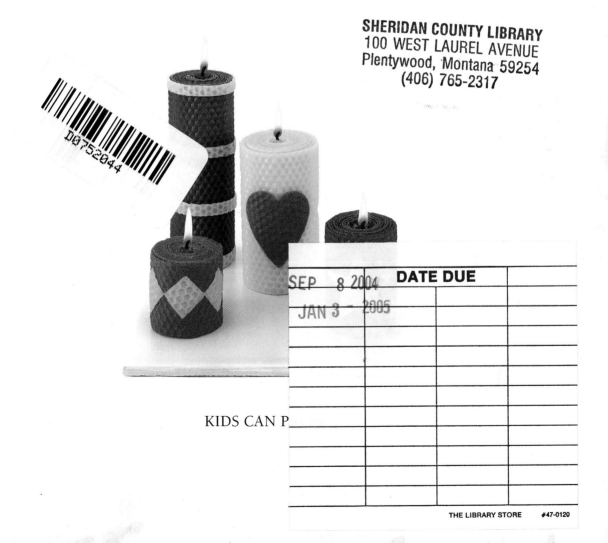

KIDS CAN P

For Carly-May, Denby and Emily,
who light up our home with
their energy, creativity, laughter and love

Text copyright © 1998 by Judy Ann Sadler
Illustrations copyright © 1998 by Tracy Walker

KIDS CAN DO IT and the 🖊 logo are trademarks of Kids Can Press Ltd.

Published in Canada by   Published in the U.S. by
Kids Can Press Ltd.   Kids Can Press Ltd.
29 Birch Avenue   85 River Rock Drive, Suite 202
Toronto, ON M4V 1E2   Buffalo, NY 14207

Edited by Elizabeth MacLeod
Designed by Karen Powers
Photographs by Frank Baldassarra
Printed in Hong Kong by Wing King Tong Co. Ltd.

CM 98 0 9 8 7 6 5 4 3 2 1

Canadian Cataloguing in Publication Data

Sadler, Judy Ann, 1959 —
Making candles

(Kids Can do it)
ISBN 1-55074-501-8

1. Candlemaking — Juvenile literature. I. Walker, Tracy.
II. Title. III. Series.

TT896.5.S23 1998   j745.593'32   C97-931629-4

3.5?/5.95   55431
Fngram   10/02

Contents

Introduction

Have you ever noticed that a lit candle in a room is the center of attention? Candlelight softens darkness in a warm, welcoming way. But it wasn't always like that! Our ancestors made tallow candles that were stinky, smoky and gave off little light. When paraffin wax and the additive stearin were developed, there was finally decent candlelight. And it wasn't much later that gas, kerosene and electricity became available. But the art of candle making has survived because candles are rich in tradition and beauty. This book shows you how to make a wide variety of candles and holders. Create candles for your home and for gift giving. And don't just use them when the electricity goes out! Burn them to make an everyday meal special. Read and tell stories by candlelight. Or enjoy the peaceful feeling you get around a flickering flame.

MATERIALS

The following materials are available around your home or at craft and hobby stores.

CANDLE WAX

You will need candle (paraffin) wax for most projects in this book. It's odorless, white and comes in bars, pellets or tiny beads (also known as shredded wax). When using bars of wax, ask an adult to help you break them apart using the point of a dull knife. You can buy wax at craft and hobby stores, and it is also usually available at grocery stores in 454 g (1 lb.) boxes, each of which contains four bars.

BEESWAX

Made by bees, this wax smells like honey. Although it is available in blocks and pellets, for the projects in this book you will need sheets of beeswax. They are available in many colors. Scraps of beeswax can be melted with candle wax to make other candles.

WICKS

Wicks are made of cotton threads specially braided together to burn well. They are available in different widths. The bigger around your candle is, the thicker the wick should be. Use a wick with a metal core for candles in large containers — the metal spreads the heat across the candle so it burns down evenly. For most candles in this book a small or medium wick will work well.

SCENTS

Add a few drops of candle scent or essential oil — perfume won't work — to your melted wax to make a scented candle. Choose a fragrance that you find pleasant or refreshing. Or use a fragrance that helps keep mosquitoes away, such as citronella.

STEARIN

This additive comes from refined animal and vegetable fats. It can make candles more opaque and help them burn longer and drip less. Stearin also makes it easier to remove candles from molds.

CANS

You'll need a different can for each color of wax you melt, so collect lots of cans, clean them and remove their labels. Save them to use over and over again.

DYES

You can use good-quality wax crayons or specially made commercial dyes to color your candles. Be sure to stir the color gently but thoroughly into the melted wax.

Before you dip into the pleasures of making candles, be sure to read the safety precautions listed on pages 6 and 7.

Basics and safety precautions

PREPARATION

• Gather together all your supplies before you begin.

• Spread waxed paper over your work area so if you spill any wax it can be peeled off and used again.

• Don't wear dangling jewelry or loose clothing that could get dipped in hot wax. If your hair is long, tie it back.

WAX SAFETY

• Wax can catch on fire if it is heated directly on a burner at very high temperatures. So always heat it in a double boiler or in a can in a small pot over medium-low heat.

• Turn the handle of the pot to the back of the stove and out of the reach of young children.

• Wear oven mitts when handling anything hot.

• Never leave melting wax unattended. If you must leave, turn off the heat and remove the pot from the stove.

• There's no reason to expect to have a fire, but for safety's sake, keep baking soda, a lid or a fire extinguisher on hand to smother a fire should it break out. Don't try to put out a fire with water.

CLEANUP

• You may need to scour the water pot after making candles. It tends to get rust stains in it from the can.

• Leftover wax should never be poured down the drain. Pour it into a bowl or tray lined with waxed paper to cool. It can be broken up and used for "chunky candles" (see page 18) or melted to make other candles.

• Spilled wax can be scraped off most surfaces. Use a dry cloth to polish away the residue it may leave on hard surfaces. If wax gets on fabric, scrape off as much as you can, then ask an adult to help you use a clean cloth and a hot iron to absorb the rest.

CANDLE STORAGE

• Store your candles away from sunshine and heat. Wrap them in waxed paper or place them in a shoebox lined with waxed paper.

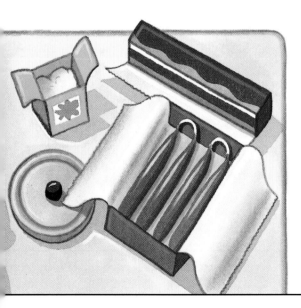

CANDLE SAFETY

• Make sure your candle is firmly held in a secure holder or, in the case of a large, thick candle, that it is on a nonflammable surface.

• Always ask for permission to light a candle. Use wooden safety matches and let them cool completely before throwing them out.

• When you are lighting a container candle that has burned down quite low or a candle in a lantern, use long wooden safety matches.

• Never leave a lit candle unattended.

• Keep matches and lit candles well out of the reach of young children.

• Place candles away from other sources of heat, such as a fireplace or space heater, and away from anything flammable.

• Never reach over lit candles — they're burning hot!

• Don't let candles burn down to the end of their wicks. Extinguish them with a candlesnuffer if you have one. If you don't, blow them out with a steady stream of air rather than a quick burst that could splatter wax.

• Keep candlewicks trimmed short so they're ready to be lit again.

> **Always ask an adult to pour any hot wax, and to help you when you are using the stove or cutting with a knife.**

Beeswax spiral candle

You'll be surprised by how quickly you can make these sweet-smelling, elegant-looking spiral candles.

YOU WILL NEED

- a sheet of beeswax
- candlewick
- waxed paper, a long ruler or straight edge, scissors, a handheld blow-dryer (optional)

1 Place the beeswax on a sheet of waxed paper. Lay the ruler on the beeswax diagonally. Use the scissors to mark a line and then cut along it. Set one triangle aside to make another candle later.

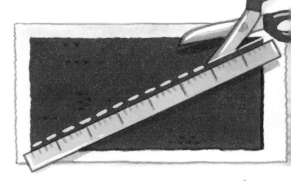

2 Cut a piece of wick about 5 cm (2 in.) longer than the shortest side of your triangle. Place the wick along the short edge of the triangle so that some of it hangs over at each end.

3 Roll and press the edge of the wax onto the wick. It helps if your hands are warm. If the wax cracks a little, press it firmly over the wick and it will stick.

4 Tightly roll the wax, keeping the straight edge even.

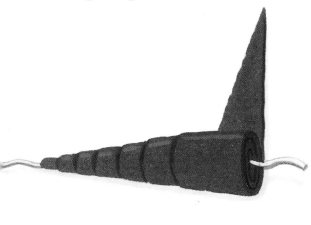

5 As you finish the candle, roll it firmly across the waxed paper to make the end stick in place. If it doesn't stick, you can warm it a little by sweeping over it with the blow-dryer.

6 Cut off the wick at the bottom of the candle and trim it to 1 cm (1/2 in.) on top. If the bottom is uneven, gently push it down on the waxed paper to make it flat.

OTHER IDEAS

• To make short candles, first cut the sheet of beeswax in half lengthwise and then cut it diagonally. Or cut straight strips and simply roll them up with a piece of wick inside.

• Try using two sheets of beeswax in different colours. Put one on top of the other and roll them together. Or roll your candle in glitter sprinkled on a sheet of waxed paper.

Beeswax pillar candle

These easy-to-make candles are especially suited to being decorated with beeswax cutouts. Press hearts, stripes, leaves, stars or other shapes onto them.

YOU WILL NEED

- 2 sheets of beeswax
- candlewick
- waxed paper, a ruler, scissors

1 On a piece of waxed paper, cut both sheets of beeswax in half lengthwise.

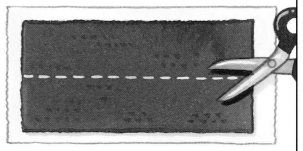

2 Cut a piece of wick about 5 cm (2 in.) longer than the short ends of the beeswax strips. Place the wick along the short end of one of the strips so that some of it hangs over at each end.

3 Roll and press the edge of the wax onto the wick. Tightly roll the wax, keeping the straight edges even.

4 When you are finished rolling the first strip, place the second one end to end with the first one and keep rolling. Continue in this way until all four pieces are rolled together. Press the end firmly onto the candle.

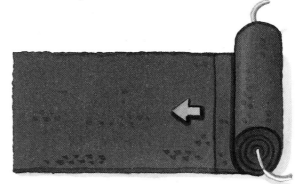

5 Cut off the wick at the bottom of the candle and trim it to 1 cm (½ in.) on top. If the bottom of the candle is uneven, gently push it down on the waxed paper to make it flat.

Beeswax cookie-cutter candle

By using cookie cutters to cut out shapes from sheets of beeswax, you can make some very interesting-looking candles.

YOU WILL NEED

- 2 to 4 sheets of beeswax
- a cookie cutter
- candlewick
- waxed paper, scissors, a handheld blow-dryer (optional)

1 On a sheet of waxed paper, use the cookie cutter to cut out at least 20 shapes from the beeswax.

2 Lay a cookie-cutter shape on the waxed paper. Cut a wick and press it into the shape. Press another shape firmly on top of it. If you find they are not sticking together, warm them a little with the blow-dryer.

3 Keep pressing on shapes, making sure you have an equal number on each side of the wick. Cut off the wick at the bottom of the candle and trim it to 1 cm (½ in.) on top. If your candle is unsteady when you stand it up, add more shapes. Decorate the candle by pressing beeswax cutouts onto it.

OTHER IDEAS

- Use small cookie cutters to make layered beeswax candles. Cut out at least 20 shapes, then use a toothpick to pierce a hole in the middle of each one. Thread a wick through the shapes one at a time, stack them and press firmly down on the shapes so they stick together.

Beeswax lighthouse candle

*When this candle is lit,
it glows like a lighthouse.*

YOU WILL NEED

- 2 or more sheets of white or very light-colored beeswax
- 1 sheet each of bright yellow and red beeswax
- candlewick
- a toothpick, waxed paper, a ruler, scissors

1 On a sheet of waxed paper, cut a piece of wick 8 cm (3 in.) longer than the short end of a sheet of beeswax. Place the wick along the short end of one of the white beeswax sheets so that it hangs evenly over each end.

2 Roll and press the edge of the wax onto the wick. Tightly roll the wax, keeping the straight edges even. When you are finished rolling the first sheet, place the second white sheet end to end with it and keep rolling. If you'd like a thicker candle, roll on another white sheet.

3 Decide which end will be the top of the candle. If the candle doesn't stand steadily, gently push and tap the bottom until it is smooth. Trim the extra wick from the bottom of the candle only.

4 Cut a strip of yellow wax about 5 cm (2 in.) wide and long enough to be wrapped around the candle. Press it firmly around the top of the candle to make the lighthouse windows.

5 Cut four very narrow strips of red wax, each 6 cm (2¼ in.) long. Place one vertically on the yellow wax so that the ends of the strip extend a little above and below the yellow wax. Press it firmly in place. Space the other narrow strips evenly around the top and press them firmly in place, too.

6 Cut enough 1 cm (½ in.) wide strips of red wax to form a band around the candle that's four layers thick. Press the strips in place below the yellow wax.

7 Cut another strip of red wax about 0.5 cm (¼ in.) wide and long enough to be wrapped around the candle. Press it firmly in place over the yellow wax at the top of the candle.

8 Cut out a circle of red wax slightly larger in diameter than your candle. Use the toothpick to poke a hole in its center. Make a cut from the edge of the circle to the center hole. Slightly overlap these cut edges and press them together to form a shallow cone.

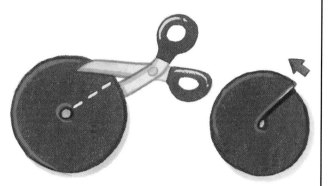

9 Thread the wick through the hole in the center of the cone. Press down on the outer edges of the cone to attach it to the top of the candle and form the roof of the lighthouse. Trim the wick to about 1 cm (½ in.).

10 Cut out two small, yellow rectangles for windows and a red, rounded door. Press them in place. Add details such as crossbars on the windows and a doorknob.

Molded candle

Many different containers can be used as candle molds. Try milk cartons; waxed-paper, Styrofoam or plastic cups; and paperboard containers from frozen juice concentrate.

YOU WILL NEED

- a medium-sized can
- candle wax, in bars or shredded
- a crayon with its paper removed
- stearin (optional)
- a small pot • candlewick
- a mold (see introduction)
- scissors, masking tape, a pencil, waxed paper, oven mitts, a spoon or stick for stirring

1 Place two bars of wax or about 500 mL (2 c.) of shredded wax, the crayon and 15 mL (1 tbsp.) of stearin (if you are using it) in the can.

2 Shape the can to form a spout. Place the can in the pot and add water to the pot until the water comes about one-third of the way up the can. If the can floats, there is too much water in the pot. Heat the pot on medium-low.

3 While the wax is melting, cut a piece of wick about 5 cm (2 in.) longer than your mold is tall. Firmly tape one end of the wick to the center bottom of the mold.

4 Place the pencil across the top of the mold and tape the top of the wick to it so that the wick is straight. Place the prepared mold on a sheet of waxed paper.

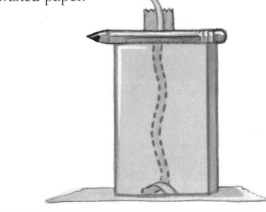

5 When the wax has melted, turn off the heat. Wearing oven mitts, remove the pot from the stove. Gently stir the wax to mix in the color.

6 Ask an adult to carefully pour the wax into the mold. Wax often shrinks as it cools, so you may want to save some wax to reheat later to top up your candle.

7 If your wick comes loose, carefully pull it out of the wax and hold it above the mold until it stops dripping. Let it cool slightly, remove the tape from the wick if it's still attached, and pull the wick straight with your fingers. Poke it back into the wax. You may need to adjust where the wick is taped to the pencil.

8 When the candle is hard and cool, trim the wick to about 1.5 cm (⅝ in.). Cut and tear away the mold.

OTHER IDEAS

• It's fun and easy to make candles by pouring wax into containers that are already decorated. Use small ornamental tins and pails (check for leaks first by pouring in water) or containers such as empty soft drink cans (with the entire top removed). Your container should not have a paper or plastic label on it. As this candle burns down, the container may get hot, so make sure it is placed on a nonflammable surface.

• Make a scented candle by adding a few drops of candle scent or essential oil. Add the scent as the wax is melting. You can add scent to almost any candle you make.

Striped candle

The first time you make this candle, try it with three colors. Later, try more layers and colors.

YOU WILL NEED

- 3 medium-sized cans
- candle wax, in bars or shredded
- 3 different-colored crayons with their papers removed
- stearin (optional)
- a small pot • candlewick
- a mold (see introduction on page 14)
- scissors, masking tape, a pencil, waxed paper, oven mitts, a spoon or stick for stirring

1 Place one bar of wax or about 250 mL (1 c.) of shredded wax, a crayon and 5 to 10 mL (1 to 2 tsp.) of stearin (if you are using it) in each can. Set two of the cans aside.

2 Follow steps 2 to 5 of "Molded candles" on pages 14–15 to melt the wax and prepare the mold.

3 Ask an adult to carefully pour the wax into the mold. (If your wick comes loose, see step 7 on page 15.) Allow this wax to cool and harden for at least an hour.

4 Melt the wax in one of the other cans and pour it over the first layer. Do the same with the third can, making sure the second stripe of color cools for at least an hour before the third layer is poured over it.

5 When the candle is finished, hard and cool, trim the wick to about 1.5 cm (⅝ in.). Cut and tear away the mold.

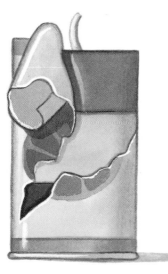

OTHER IDEAS

• Try making a candle with slanted stripes. Before you begin, find a secure spot, such as an egg carton, small bowl or large cup, where you can set your mold on a slant while the wax cools.

Prepare your mold as you would for a regular striped candle. You will need to fasten the pencil to the mold so that the wick stays straight. To do this, stretch a rubber band around the mold and pencil or tape the pencil to the sides of the mold.

Pour in melted wax, set the mold securely on an angle and allow the wax to harden. Melt a different-colored wax and pour it in. Place the mold on a different angle and allow this layer of wax to harden.

Continue in this way until you have as many slanted layers as you like, but be sure to end with a straight layer. Trim the wick and remove the mold.

Chunky candle

This candle has a soft, stained-glass look when it is burning.

1 Depending on the size of your mold, place at least two bars of wax or 500 mL (2 c.) of shredded wax in the can. Don't add color to the wax.

2 Shape the can to form a spout. Place the can in the pot and add water to the pot until the water comes about one-third of the way up the can. Heat the pot on medium-low.

3 While the wax is melting, ask an adult to help you break and cut up the chunks of wax. Remove any wicks from the candle stubs.

4 Cut a piece of wick about 5 cm (2 in.) longer than your mold is tall. Tape one end to the center bottom of the mold.

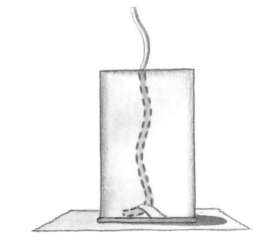

5 Place the pencil across the top of the mold and tape the top of the wick to it so that the wick is straight.

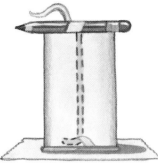

6 Pack the mold with wax chunks, placing them all around the wick. Make sure the wick stays in the center.

7 When the wax in the can has melted, turn off the heat. Wearing oven mitts, remove the pot from the stove. Ask an adult to carefully pour the wax over the chunks in the mold. If you like, leave some of the chunks sticking out at the top.

8 Allow the wax to cool and harden. Trim the wick to about 1.5 cm (⅝ in.). Cut and tear away the mold.

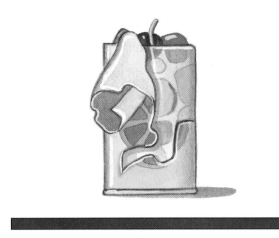

OTHER IDEAS

• Instead of packing the mold with chunks of wax, pack it with different-sized pieces of ice. Be sure to wait to fill the mold with ice until just before you're ready to pour in the melted wax so the ice doesn't melt. When the candle is cool and hard, hold it over the sink as you tear away the mold, since water from the melted ice will flow out.

Clay-pot candle

*This project is a candle and holder
all in one. Make it as plain
or as fancy as you like.*

YOU WILL NEED

- a clean, dry clay pot, 5 to 9 cm
  (2 to 3 1/2 in.) in diameter
- newspaper, acrylic craft paint
  and a paintbrush (optional)
- a can
- candle wax, in bars or shredded
- a crayon with its paper removed
- a small pot   • candlewick
- scissors, a pencil, masking tape,
  waxed paper, oven mitts

1 If you are going to paint your pot,
spread newspaper over your work
surface. See "Other ideas" on the facing
page for some suggestions on how to
paint it. You don't need to paint the
inside of the pot, except for the rim.
Allow the pot to dry completely.

2 Place one or two bars of wax or
250 to 500 mL (1 to 2 c.) of
shredded wax and the crayon in the can.

3 Shape the can to form a spout.
Place the can in the pot and add
water to the pot until the water comes
about one-third of the way up the can.
Heat the pot on medium-low.

4 While the wax is melting, stick at least two layers of masking tape inside the pot, across the hole in the bottom. Cut a piece of wick about 5 cm (2 in.) longer than your pot is tall. Tape the wick to the center bottom of the pot.

5 Place the pencil across the top of the clay pot and tape the top of the wick to it so that the wick is straight. Place the prepared pot on a sheet of waxed paper.

6 When the wax has melted, turn off the heat. Wearing oven mitts, remove the pot from the stove. Gently stir the wax to mix in the color.

7 Ask an adult to carefully pour the wax into the clay pot to about 1 cm (½ in.) from the top. If the wax shrinks as it hardens, fill in the hollow with a bit more melted wax. Trim the wick to about 1.5 cm (⅝ in.).

OTHER IDEAS

• When you add color to your candle, choose a color to match the paint or decorations on your pot.

• For a festive clay pot, paint the pot gold on the outside and around the rim on the inside. Add color and a scent and sprinkle a little gold glitter on top of the wax as it hardens.

• Instead of painting the pot, tie on a bow or glue on fabric, rhinestones or other trimmings. Make sure the decorations will not be near the flame.

• Instead of pouring wax directly into a clay pot, decorate a pot and use it as a candleholder. Sponge paint your pot or paint on dots, stripes, squiggles or geometric shapes. You can also use dimensional fabric paint to draw on designs. How about painting a pot white and giving it cow- or Dalmatian-style spots? It would look great with a red candle. Before you place a candle in your clay-pot candleholder, line the bottom of the pot with foil to cover the hole.

Egg candle

*You'll want to make these
candles by the dozen!
Use an eggcup for a holder.*

YOU WILL NEED

- an egg carton
- eggs, any number
- a clean, large, sharp needle or pin
- a bowl
- a can
- candle wax, in bars or shredded
- a small pot
- candlewick
- vegetable oil
- a crayon with its paper removed
- a ruler, scissors, oven mitts, a spoon or stick for stirring

1 Place an egg in the carton, pointed end up, and poke a hole in the shell with the needle. Chip away some of the shell to make a hole about 2 cm (¾ in.) across. Break up the yolk with the needle and then pour the white and yolk into the bowl. Remove the whitish lining from the inside of the shell. Thoroughly rinse out the shell and place it upside down to dry. Repeat this process with all the eggs you are using.

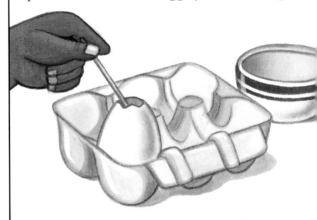

2 Two bars of wax or 500 mL (2 c.) of shredded wax will fill about six eggs. Keeping this in mind, place as much wax as you'll need in the can, along with a crayon.

3 Shape the can to form a spout. Place the can in the pot and add water to the pot until the water comes about one-third of the way up the can. Heat the pot on medium-low.

4 While the wax is melting, thoroughly coat the insides of the dry eggshells with vegetable oil. Place them upright in the egg carton.

5 Cut a length of wick long enough for all your eggs. You will need about 8 cm (3 in.) for each egg.

6 When the wax has melted, turn off the heat. Remove the pot from the stove. Ask an adult to very carefully dip the length of wick into the wax. Hold it above the can until it stops dripping.

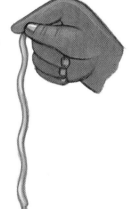

7 Hold one end of the wick in each hand, pull it straight and hold it as it cools. Cut it into 8 cm (3 in.) pieces when it has hardened.

8 Ask an adult to carefully pour the wax into the prepared eggs. As the wax begins to set but is still soft (after about ten minutes), poke a prepared wick into each egg.

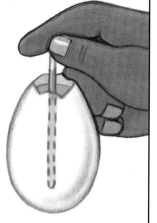

9 As the wax cools it will shrink and leave a hollow in each egg. Heat more wax to fill the hollow spaces. When the wax is hard and cool, peel off the shells. If areas of the shells are difficult to peel off, firmly tap them on the countertop.

OTHER IDEAS

• If you want to leave your candle in its shell, don't oil the inside of the egg or peel off the shell. You can also make smaller egg candles this way, using shells that have been cracked in half. You may even want to decorate the shells with water paints or acrylic craft paints, or try dyeing them.

• For shiny egg candles, polish the finished candles with a little vegetable oil.

• Make candles in seashells. Be sure the shells are steady and won't wobble.

Floating cookie-cutter candle

These lovely, little candles look pretty floating in a bowl of water, whether or not they're lit.

YOU WILL NEED

- a medium-sized can
- candle wax, in bars or shredded
- a crayon with its paper removed
- a small pot
- small, deep cookie cutters
- vegetable oil
- modeling clay, such as Plasticine
- candlewick
- waxed paper, scissors, oven mitts, a spoon or stick for stirring

1 Depending on the size and number of your cookie cutters, place about two bars of wax or 500 mL (2 c.) of shredded wax into the can along with the crayon.

2 Shape the can to form a spout. Place the can in the pot and add water to the pot until the water comes about one-third of the way up the can. Heat the pot on medium-low.

3 Use your fingers to lightly coat the inside of each cookie cutter with vegetable oil. Place them on two layers of waxed paper.

4 Use the modeling clay to thoroughly seal around the base of each cutter. If your cookie cutters are made from metal and have seams, carefully seal the seams on the outside.

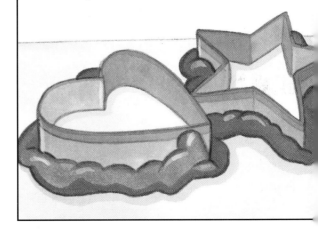

5 Ask an adult to very carefully dip a length of wick into the melting wax. Allow it to drip over the can. When the wick is no longer hot, pull it on both ends until it is cool, hard and straight. Cut it into pieces that are 2 cm (¾ in.) longer than your cookie cutters are tall.

6 When the wax has melted, turn off the heat. Wearing oven mitts, remove the pot from the stove. Gently stir the wax to mix the color.

7 Ask an adult to carefully pour the wax into the cookie-cutter molds. Save some wax for topping up the candles later.

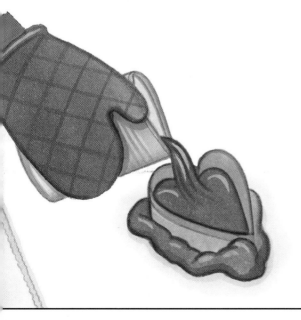

8 When the wax is starting to set but is still soft, poke a prepared wick into the middle of each cookie cutter. (If the wick doesn't stand up straight, place a pencil across the top of each cookie cutter to hold it upright.) Allow the wax to cool and harden for at least an hour. Heat the leftover wax and top up the candles.

9 When the candles are completely hard and cool, lift them off the waxed paper. Remove the modeling clay.

10 To release the candles from the molds, you may need to pull at the sides of the cookie cutters. Trim the wicks to about 1 cm (½ in.), if necessary.

OTHER IDEAS

• Wax naturally floats, so any short, wide candle you make will float in a bowl of water. Try making candles in foil tart or cupcake pans, or in the bases of small plastic soft drink bottles or disposable cups. Follow the instructions for "Molded candles" (see page 14) to make them.

Floating water lily

This wax water lily floating in a glass bowl makes a beautiful table centerpiece for a party.

YOU WILL NEED

- 1 sheet each of yellow, white and green beeswax
- candlewick
- ruler, scissors, a paring knife, a handheld blow-dryer (optional)

1 Cut a 5 cm (2 in.) wide strip from one long side of the yellow sheet of beeswax.

2 Cut an 8 cm (3 in.) piece of wick. Place it on the short end of the yellow strip so that some of it hangs over at each end. Tightly roll the strip into a short candle. Set it aside.

3 From the white sheet of beeswax, cut four petal shapes each 6 cm (2¼ in.) long and four petal shapes each 9 cm (3½ in.) long.

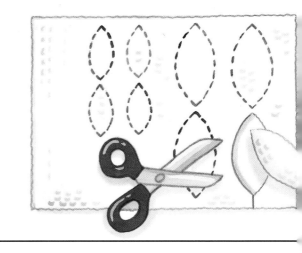

4 Wrap the base of each small petal around the base of the yellow candle. Then wrap the large petals around it. Gently bend back the tips of the petals.

6 Push the base of the flower candle through the center of the lily pad. Don't worry if the center tears a little. Press the lily pad around the candle base and gently shape it into the form of a shallow bowl.

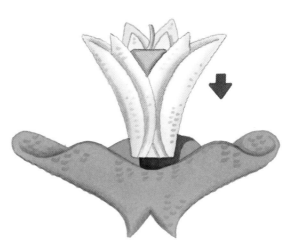

5 From the green sheets of beeswax, cut a circle about 20 cm (8 in.) across. To make it look like a lily pad, cut indents all around the edge of it. In the center, cut an **X** about 3 cm (1¼ in.) across.

7 Press the candle, petals and lily pad together firmly. If they don't stick together, use the blow-dryer to warm the wax. Cut off the wick at the bottom and trim it to 1 cm (½ in.) on top.

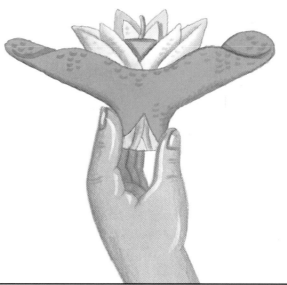

Frosted cupcake candle

This candle is a treat to make. See the "Other ideas" section to find out how to make a mug of hot chocolate to go with it!

YOU WILL NEED

- 2 cans
- candle wax, in bars or shredded
- a brown crayon with its paper removed
- a small pot • candlewick
- a foil cupcake or tart cup • a fork
- a plastic margarine or yogurt tub
- additional pieces of crayons
- grater, vegetable peeler or paring knife
- scissors, masking tape, a pencil, waxed paper, oven mitts, a spoon or stick for stirring

1 Place one bar of wax or about 250 mL (1 c.) of shredded wax and half the brown crayon in one of the cans. Follow steps 2 to 5 of "Molded candles" (page 14) to make the cupcake portion of this candle. The foil cup will be your mold.

2 Ask an adult to carefully pour the brown wax into the foil cup. Since this candle will have "frosting," you don't need to top it up.

3 When the candle is cool and hard, remove the pencil but do not trim the wick. Carefully remove the candle from the mold and trim the bottom wick.

4 Melt a smaller amount of wax in the other can for the frosting. If you'd like colored frosting, add a very small piece of crayon.

5 Ask an adult to carefully pour a little of the melted wax into the margarine tub. Allow it to cool for a few minutes until a thin coating forms on top. Use the fork to beat the wax; scrape the sides of the container often.

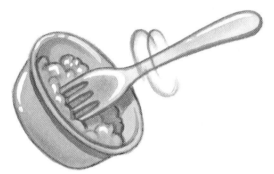

6 When the wax is frothy, quickly spread it onto the cupcake candle. Make sure the wick does not get covered. Whip more wax if you need it. If the wax hardens before you get a chance to spread it, return it to the melting can and begin again.

7 Before the frosting hardens, grate a little of the rest of the brown crayon over the candle to make chocolate sprinkles on the cupcake. Trim the wick if necessary.

OTHER IDEAS

• How about a mug of hot chocolate to go with that cupcake? Make a molded candle (see page 14) in a coffee mug and top it with white wax "whipping cream." Sprinkle on "chocolate" and a bit of (real) cinnamon. Yum!

Dipped candle

Dipped candles have been made for centuries. These instructions show you how to make two at once.

YOU WILL NEED

- a crayon with its paper removed
- 8 bars (about 907 g or 2 lb.) of candle wax
- about 50 mL (¼ c.) stearin (optional)
- a tall 1.36 L (48 oz.) juice can
- a small pot
- 2 chairs
- candlewick
- a ruler
- masking tape, scissors, a spoon or stick for stirring, a paring knife

1 Place the crayon and some of the wax in the can. Place the can in the pot and add water to the pot until the water comes about one-third of the way up the can, but be sure that the pot is no more than half-full of water.

2 Heat the pot on medium-low. As the wax melts, carefully add more wax and the stearin (if you are using it) until all of it is melted. The melted wax should be at least 4 cm (1½ in.) from the top of the can. It may take over half an hour for all the wax to melt.

3 Place two chairs close together, back to back, near where you are working.

4 Cut a piece of wick 43 cm (17 in.) long. Center and tape it over the middle of the ruler.

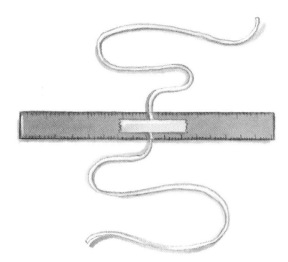

5 When all the wax has melted, turn the heat down to low. Ask an adult to very carefully stir the wax to mix in the color. Hold one end of the ruler and dip the wicks into the wax. Hold the ruler and wicks above the wax until they stop dripping.

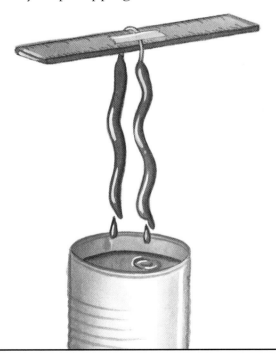

6 Place the ruler across the backs of the chairs so the wicks hang down in between them. Gently pull on the wicks to straighten them. Allow them to cool for one to two minutes.

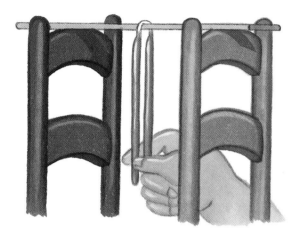

7 Dip the wicks into the wax again. Allow them to drip, then hang and straighten them between the chairs and allow them to cool. Repeat this step until the wicks stay straight.

8 Continue dipping the wicks straight down into the wax and straight back up in one smooth, unhurried movement. Make sure the end of the wick goes to the bottom of the can.

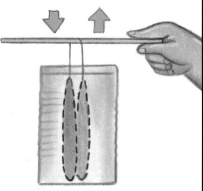

Instructions continue on the next page ☞

9 Allow the wicks to cool for one to two minutes between dips. You will likely need to dip them 20 to 30 times, depending on how thick you want your candles to be. As they get thicker, be careful that they don't touch as you dip and hang them.

10 When you have finished your candles, turn off the stove. Hang the candles and allow them to dry overnight (or see page 33 for how to make twisted candles). Before you burn the candles, cut them apart and trim the wicks. You may also need to trim off any drips on the bottoms so you can fit them in candleholders. Ask an adult to help you trim them with a paring knife.

(or see page 33 for how to make twisted candles)

OTHER IDEAS

• To make rainbow candles, start by making one or more pairs of candles using white wax.

Then stir a light-colored crayon, such as yellow or pink, into the wax, but don't dip the whole length of the candles into it.

Add a darker color and dip again, but not the whole candle.

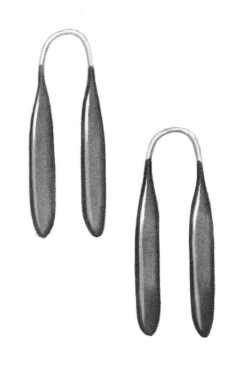

• Make a few pairs of candles at the same time. Tape more pieces of wick to other rulers and take turns dipping the different pairs of candles. You will need to add more wax to the can as the level gets low.

Twisted candle

You will likely find that these look best if you use candles that are not too thick — ones dipped 15 to 20 times work well.

YOU WILL NEED

- freshly dipped, warm candles (see pages 30–32)
- a rolling pin
- scissors, waxed paper

1 Cut the wick that joins your candles and place one candle on a sheet of waxed paper. Fold the waxed paper over it.

2 Starting about 2.5 cm (1 in.) from the bottom of your candle, use the rolling pin to firmly press and partially flatten it.

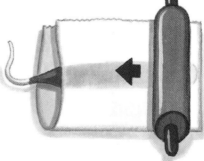

3 Hold one end of the candle in each hand. Slowly twist the ends in opposite directions to form the twists. Roll and twist the other candle.

4 Allow the candles to cool and harden by hanging them up or placing them on waxed paper.

Painting candles

Decorate homemade or store-bought candles to make one-of-a-kind works of art. Cover your work surface with newspaper or plastic before you begin.

YOU WILL NEED

- a sponge
- scissors
- a plain candle
- a small plate or candleholder
- acrylic craft paint
- a paint tray, such as a foil pie plate or a Styrofoam tray

1 Cut out a small, simple shape from the sponge.

2 If your candle can stand on its own, place it on the small plate. Otherwise, fit it into a candleholder.

3 Pour a small amount of paint into your tray. Dip the sponge shape in the paint, then dab off any extra paint on an unused area of the tray.

4 Lightly press the sponge onto the candle. You can create a pattern on your candle or print wherever you like. Turn the candleholder as you work to paint all sides of the candle.

5 If you wish to change paint colors, thoroughly rinse the sponge and dip it into another color of paint. Allow the paint to dry completely before you burn the candle.

OTHER IDEAS

• Rather than cutting out a shape from the sponge, cut off a small piece of it to lightly sponge-paint the entire candle. When the first color is dry, sponge another color over it, and another color after that if you wish.

• Use a brush to paint on polka dots, stripes and zigzags, or to paint on any other design or scene. If you find the paint doesn't stick to the candle very well, mix it with one or two drops of liquid dish detergent.

Glass-jar lantern

Use a glass jar with an interesting shape, or a plain one that you can decorate. The wire handle makes it perfect for hanging indoors or out.

YOU WILL NEED

- a medium-sized glass jar with a screw-on lid
- dimensional fabric paint
- 20 gauge wire (available at hardware stores)
- a ruler
- pliers with a wire cutter

1 Remove the label from the jar and thoroughly wash and dry the jar. If there is glue on it from the label, try removing it with nail polish remover.

2 Use the paint to draw a picture or interesting designs on the jar. This paint is not permanent on glass, so if you make a mistake, let the paint dry, peel it off and begin again. Allow your artwork to dry for a few hours or overnight.

3 Wrap the wire once around the neck of the jar, then add 12 cm (4¾ in.) and cut a piece of wire this length. Ask an adult to help you use the pliers to twist the ends of the wire together to form a secure circle.

4 Place the wire circle around the neck of the jar so that the twisted-together ends are at the back.

6 To make the handle, cut another piece of wire about 50 cm (20 in.) long. Ask an adult to help you use the pliers to fasten the ends of the wire onto the loops on the jar.

5 Pinch together the extra wire to form a small loop on each side of the jar. Use your thumbs and index fingers to twist these loops in opposite directions from each other. Twist the loops around two or three times until the wire is circling the neck of the jar very tightly. Bend the loops upward.

7 This is a good lantern to hold a short, molded candle that you've made. Ask an adult to help you light the candle, drip a few drops of wax into the jar, blow out the candle and place it in the wax puddle. This will hold the candle in place.

8 A candle in this type of lantern should be lit with a long wooden safety match. After you've blown out the candle, screw on the lid until the next time you wish to use your glass-jar lantern.

Plaster candleholder

Some candles in this book are large enough to stand on their own. Others, such as the spiral beeswax and dipped candles, need candleholders.

YOU WILL NEED

- a small glass dessert dish or shallow can
- a plastic margarine or yogurt tub
- casting plaster, such as plaster of paris
- a slender candle
- decorations (see step 8)
- a spoon, waxed paper, a rubber band, a Popsicle stick

1 Fill the glass dish about three-quarters full of water. Pour this water into the margarine tub.

2 Spoon or pour some plaster into the margarine tub. Add enough to make a thick, creamy mixture. Stir it until there are no lumps.

3 Pour the plaster mixture into the dish until the dish is about three-quarters full.

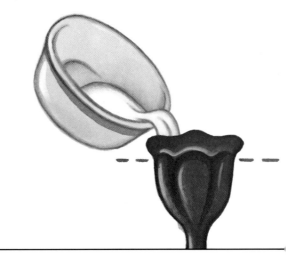

4 Wrap the bottom of your candle in waxed paper. Use the rubber band to secure the waxed paper close to the candle.

5 To check how the plaster in the dish is setting, test it every few minutes with the Popsicle stick. When it has started to set, push the wrapped candle into its center, right to the bottom of the dish. Make sure the rubber band stays above the plaster.

6 Make sure the candle is straight as you hold it in place for a few minutes until the plaster thickens.

7 Depending on the type of plaster you are using, it will take anywhere from a couple of hours to a day or more for the plaster to harden. When it is hard, remove the candle and waxed paper. You may need to let the area around the hole dry some more.

8 Paint the plaster with acrylic craft paint or glue on glitter, sequins, buttons or beads. Decorate the outside of the candleholder by gluing on rhinestones, sequins, shells, beads or buttons, or by painting it.

9 When you use this holder, you may need to wrap the bottom of your candle in foil to hold it securely in place. Extinguish the candle before it burns down to the plaster.

More candleholders

CANS

Shallow cans or large metal jar lids make good candleholders. Use dimensional fabric paint to decorate them. Or ask an adult to help you use a glue gun to fasten on beads, buttons, shells or sequins. Make sure the decorations are out of the way of the candle flame. Add feet to your candleholder by gluing four evenly spaced beads to the bottom of the can.

JARS

Decorate tall jars by using raffia to tie on fresh leaves, cinnamon sticks and twigs. Make sure nothing you tie on is higher than the top of the jar. Half-fill the jars with damp sand. Place a short pillar or other sturdy candle in each. This candleholder looks great outside, where the jar will protect the candle flame from breezes.

NATURAL HOLDERS

Try coring a large apple to hold a tall candle. If the base of the apple is unsteady, cut a slice off its bottom. Gourds, pumpkins and oranges are other natural candleholders you can make. Place them on a nonflammable surface, such as a plate. These holders are for one-time use only.

OTHER HOLDERS

Cut-glass tumblers, odd cups and saucers, eggcups, flat rocks, ceramic tiles and store-bought holders can all be used to show off your candles.